ABOUT MY

FATHER'S

BUSINESS

TAKING YOUR FAITH TO WORK

REGI CAMPBELL

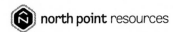

north point resources

Multnomah*Publishers *Sisters, Oregon*

About My Father's Business Small Group Study Guide

©2005 by Regi Campbell / About My Father's Business

International Standard Book Number: 1-59052-628-7

Scripture quotations are from:

The Holy Bible, New International Version
©1973, 1984 by International Bible Society,
used by permission of Zondervan Publishing House.

Printed in the United States of America

For information:

About My Father's Business

www.amfb.com

05 06 07 08 09 10 - 10 9 8 7 6 5 4 3 2 1 0

TABLE of CONTENTS

Introduction
5

Week 1 — Work, Calling, and the
Next Step in the "Purpose-Driven Life"
7

Week 2 — *Intentionality*
21

Week 3 — *Relationships are the Thing!*
41

Week 4 — *Going on the Journey with Them!*
51

Week 5 — *Taking Them on a Journey with You!*
63

Week 6 — *From "It" to "Him"*
73

Week 7 — *The Excelling Christian . . . At Work*
85

Intentionality Map — *IMAP*
95

Leader's Guide
97

ABOUT MY
FATHER'S
BUSINESS

*Y*ou are about to embark on one of the most significant journeys
that you will ever take . . . making your work into something
that is "God-centered." It's huge! It can make every day an adventure,
every relationship a positive challenge, and every encounter with someone
at work an opportunity.

Most of us work at a job every day. Most Americans who are
physically able and who either have to or choose to, work. A small
percentage can afford to retire, or to only work part time.

So since we were designed by our Creator to work, and most of us do
it, why are so few of us happy and fulfilled in our work? The secret lies
in the "why" we go to work. Seven weeks from now, we'll have a clear
answer to the "why" question as well as a process that will help us to
know "how" as well.

We'll begin by looking at our workplace and how we know that we're
supposed to take on two jobs at the same time . . . the job that brings in
a paycheck AND the job that Jesus gave us when he said "Go make
disciples."

Our next priority will be to examine ourselves and see what we need to do to become useful as a "special agent for God" in the "work nation." One of our first looks will be into the mirror. Where am I in my spiritual life? What's my story? Am I ready and willing to tell it to the people that I work with?

Then, we'll explore ways to effectively interact with the people in our workplace for the purpose of influencing them toward Christ. We'll dig into the Scriptures to see what God has to say about our interactions with others, and we'll examine the model for our behavior, Jesus Christ, and how he interacted with people in his sphere of influence. And we'll finish by learning about people's sensitivities . . . some of the more subtle points of building relationships with "outsiders."

That's what we'll be exploring over the next seven weeks. What am I supposed to do? Where do I fit in? How do I change what I do from 9 to 5 each day to make a difference for Christ?

There is no greater encouragement . . . no sense of fulfillment . . . nothing more enjoyable than knowing what God has called you to do. And then to know that you're doing it.

That sounds pretty good! Let's go firm it up.

WORK, CALLING AND THE NEXT STEP IN THE "PURPOSE-DRIVEN LIFE"

Read Pages 13-29 in *About My Father's Business*

Principles and Truths for this week

1. Christianity is both a blessing and a calling. When we stop with the blessing . . . what we'll call "phase I" or the "I" focused part of Christianity, we miss the calling and the opportunity to have true purpose and meaning in life, which comes with "others focused" Christianity ("phase II").

2. All Christians are called to "make disciples". . . it's not someone else's job.

3. Work is our assigned mission field; it's not "second class" and it's no less sacred a calling than being a pastor.

4. The "purpose driven life" is about "glorifying God." We must do that at work by . . .

   a. Being "His"

   b. Being respected

   c. Being intentional

Memory Verse for Week One

"In the same way, let your light shine before men, that they may see your good deeds and praise your Father in heaven."
MATTHEW 5:16

Rate Yourself (Be Kind!)

If you were sitting in a conference room and the speaker asked you to take out a piece of paper and rate yourself as an "evangelist" or as a "disciple maker," how would you rate yourself? 10? 5? 2?

Most of us would have a hard time giving ourselves high marks. To begin with, the "bar" has been set so high that we don't feel that we could ever jump over it. We've heard about the guy who leads people to Christ on airplanes, and he does it one after another. We've never done that, and have no vision for how we ever could.

We've also defined "evangelism" wrongly. We think of it as an event rather than a process. And since we have no skill or experience in making those "events" happen, we feel bad about ourselves and withdraw from the process altogether.

Over the next few weeks, we want to clear up those wrong perceptions. Influencing people toward Christ is a process, not an event. It's a team effort that many people play small roles in, but together has huge impact. And just being "on the team" and being involved may be the most satisfying and fulfilling part of being a Christian. The process that we're going to learn will make evangelism and discipleship *doable* for you! Instead of being a source of frustration and feeling like a failure, you are going to get excited and energized about making a difference for Christ in the work "nation."

The instruction that Jesus gave to "go into every nation and make disciples" is one that we've all heard. Some of us have "glossed over" those verses, assuming they were directed to someone else at some other time in some other place. Others have a full load of guilt on their backs, knowing that the words were spoken by Jesus and directed to them, but they've never acted on the instruction, never tried to make a disciple, and never shared their faith with anyone, ever. In between these two extremes fall the rest of us. We "sort of" know that we're supposed to make disciples; we "sort of" know what that means, and we "sort of" try to, now and again, but we don't know what we're doing and we don't think we're very good at it. This week, we're going to get clear and specific about our calling to "make disciples."

And just what is a disciple?

A learner and follower of Jesus Christ! When we are about our Father's business, we are learners and followers of Jesus Christ and we are intentional about leading others to be disciples also.

Jesus' instruction was clear and specific, spoken after His resurrection, and recorded by all four of the gospel writers, as well as the writer of the book of Acts.

Read each of the following verses. Record the instruction that Jesus gave in each verse below.

Matthew 28:19 *go + make disciples of all nations, baptizing them in the name of the Father and of the son and of the H.S.*

Mark 16:15 *Go into all the world and preach the good news to all creation*

Luke 24:47 *and repentance + forgiveness of sins will be preached in his name to all nations beginning at Jerusalem.*

John 20:21 *Again Jesus said, "Peace be with you! And as the Father has sent me, I am sending you."*

Acts 1:8 *But you will receive power when the H.S. comes on you; and you will be my*

"Go" and "make" says "initiate"—start a creative process within someone; a process that will create a disciple! All "nations" includes our work "nation." It's a place with its own culture, its own rules and laws, its own language, and even its own social order. We are to "initiate" the process that will create disciples in the work "nation," just as a missionary to a foreign country would.

"Baptizing" indicates a rebirth. Leading people to rebirth is a part of "repentance and forgiveness of sins." "Preaching" says we intentionally communicate for the purpose of salvation. "Being sent" confirms that there is a "sender." We have a Master who is sending us, and we are obeying that Master, not just coming up with good things to do for God. And "be my witnesses" says that we must simply tell people what we have seen ourselves… what we have seen Jesus do in our own lives. Finally, "to the ends of the earth" certainly includes our work environments, which is the focus of this study.

Work is Our "Nation"

Like it or not, work is its own "nation" of sorts. It has its own culture, its own language, its own social structure and its own set of laws, rules and regulations. Only recently have Christians begun to see that this work "nation" is ripe for the gospel, and that we who "journey" there every day have a golden opportunity to influence that nation for Christ.

witnesses in Jerusalem, and in all Judea and Samaria, and to the ends of the earth.

Our "Paying Job"

Regardless of our position or industry, we all are workers. Because work is hard, most of us think of it as a curse… something to be endured. But that isn't Biblical truth. Check out Genesis 2:15—

> *"The LORD God took the man and put him in the Garden of Eden to work it and take care of it."*

Note that the fall of man didn't happen until later, in chapter 3, verse 6. And then in verse 18, when God is describing the consequences of man's rebellion against Him, He tells men that their work will now be "painful toil."

So work, in and of itself, isn't a curse. We were made to work. It is unnatural and debilitating to do nothing. Without work, we become like a fine car that never gets driven. We atrophy . . . we become a museum piece and we fall short of our intended purpose.

The key is to have *purpose* in our work . . . a reason to work in addition to the reason of earning money. To go further, it's actually a *more important* reason to work than earning money. It's an *eternal* reason!

Rick Warren's book, *The Purpose Driven Life*, convinces us that our purpose in life, including in our work life, is to glorify God. But how? How do we do that?

The word "glorify" can be interchanged with the word "praise." God wants us to live our lives in such a way that we are a "praise" to Him. Whatever we do or say, however we act, wherever we go, our words and actions . . . even our thoughts are a "praise" to Him. He's proud of them, just as a dad is proud of every good word or action of his child.

Glorifying God with our Lives

So how do we live a life that praises God every day at work? We're going to look at three fundamentals of a work life that praises God, and empowers us to "go and make disciples."

1. Be His . . . We must first insure that we have been adopted into God's family and that we have a solid relationship with the Father. Read the section headed "Your Relationship with Christ" on pages 47-49, and then answer the following questions.

List three words that describe your life (before) you trusted Christ.

independent, self-sufficient

Describe, in three or four sentences, the circumstances that drove you to need the Lord in your life.

Again, in three or four sentences, detail what happened in the 24 hours surrounding your committing your life to Christ.

paradigm shift

how to answer every one.

List three words that describe your life *since* you trusted Christ with your life.

less fear

What you have just written is the basic "skeleton" of your story . . . your "testimony", to use a big church word. We'll come back to your story several times over the next weeks.

2. Be Respected . . . If you decide to be "about your Father's business" in the workplace, you will only be effective if you are respected in the culture of the work "nation." Just as any missionary who is assigned to carry Christ to another culture, you must know the "rules of the road" in that culture so that you can earn the respect of the people there, and ultimately gain influence with them. As usual, God has given us the answers to earning that respect in his Word. Read the following verses and learn 9 keys to earning respect at work.

A. Proverbs 22:29 *Do you see a man skilled in his work? He will serve before kings; he will not serve before obscure men.*

B. Phil. 2:14 *Do everything without complaining or arguing*

C. Col. 4:1 *Masters, provide your slaves with what is right and fair, because you know that you also have a Master in heaven.*

D. Col. 4:5-6 *Be wise in the way you act toward outsiders; make the most of every opportunity. Let your conversation be always full of grace, seasoned with salt, so that you may know*

E. I Thess. 4:12 *so that your daily life may win the respect of outsiders and so that you will not be dependent on anybody.*

F. Col. 3:22-25 *Slaves, obey your earthly masters in everything; and do it, not only when their eye is on you and to win their favor, but with sincerity of heart & reverence for the Lord.*

G. Eccl. 9:10 *whatever your hand finds to do, do it with all your might.*

H. Matt. 5:37 *Simply let your "yes" be "yes" and your "no", "No"; anything beyond this comes from the evil one.*

I. Phil 2:3-4 *Do nothing out of selfish ambition or*

vain conceit, but in humility consider others better than yourselves. Each of you should look not only to your own interests, but also to the interests of others.

> "Now Daniel so distinguished himself among the
> administrators and the satraps by his exceptional qualities
> that the king planned to set him over the whole kingdom."
> DANIEL 6:3

We will have limited influence at work for Christ unless we distinguish ourselves as great workers. But if these qualities become descriptive of who we are at work, we can achieve great success in our jobs, and that will enable us to have influence as "ministers" as well!

3. Be intentional . . . When we first become committed Christians, we are giddy with our new-found faith and all the benefits of our new relationship with Christ.

"*I* have peace, *I* have forgiveness, *I* have purpose, *I* have a perfect Father who loves and protects *me*." "*I* have great new friends, *I* have a church, with people there who love *me* and care about *me*!" "*I* have the Bible . . . a dependable 'operator's manual' for life." "*I* have a promise that *I'll* live forever in heaven."

14

Whatever you do, work at it with all your heart, as working for the Lord, not for men, since you know that you will receive an inheritance from the Lord as a reward. It is the Lord Christ you are serving.

All true, and granted it's all good stuff!

But count how many "I's" are in that paragraph! It's all about me and what I *get* from God. This is what I call "phase I" Christianity, and it's where most of us have stopped and camped out. It's why so many Christians and the churches they attend are so weak and lifeless.

Jesus calls us to "phase II" Christianity. He wants us to make the move from "me centered" Christianity to the "others centered" life that He modeled for us.

Read Matthew 16:24 and answer the following:

1. If "anyone" comes after Jesus, where will he/she end up?
   Where is Jesus today? *with Jesus and his angels coming in His kingdom ... then He will reward each person according to what he has done*

2. How does the concept of "denying yourself" lay down with the "I" focus of "phase I" Christianity?

   Cease to make self the object of his life and actions

3. What do you think "take up your cross" means?

   necessity of total commitment — even unto death — on the part of Jesus' disciples

4. How do you interpret "follow me" as it relates to the "work nation"?

Given the direct order to "deny ourselves, take up our cross, and follow Him," we're not given the choice to just stay focused on ourselves. While it's comfortable to be quiet about our faith; to stay passive and to "run and hide" when issues come up at work . . . it's just not what Jesus told us to do!

So, to *be intentional* means to move from passive to active, from "phase I" Christianity, where it's all about me, to "phase II" Christianity where it's about others. God wants us to be focused on Him and on others. He called this "the greatest commandment" and "the second is like it," in Matthew 22:37-39:

> *Jesus replied: "'Love the Lord your God with all your heart and with all your soul and with all your mind.' This is the first and greatest commandment. And the second is like it: 'Love your neighbor as yourself.'"*

Intentionality means being on purpose in everything we do. We're focused on God all the time. We're constantly talking to Him, acknowledging His presence, thanking Him for what just happened, asking His advice on how to respond to the people and the situation at hand, asking Him for courage to take a risk, asking Him for the strength to "stay in the game" and not give up. We need His grace to accept people who aren't pulling their weight. We need His presence to willingly forgive the person who lied to us about something at work, even when that lie cost us something.

You see, intentionality is about motive, and God wants our motives to be about loving Him and about loving others. That's living a life that's a "praise" to Him in every dimension. That's selflessness. That's being single minded, with the focus of "all your heart," "all your soul," and "all your mind" being about Him.

Being "about our Father's business" adds a spiritual dimension to everything we do and to every work relationship. It says that we are to love and serve each person that we encounter at work so that we can ultimately help them take their next step toward Christ, regardless of what that step is. We'll begin by getting to know them well enough that we discover what they believe. We'll pray for them and over time, God may just use us in some small way to influence them toward an exciting relationship with the Father.

So let's summarize what we've covered so far . . .

1. Being a disciple…a "learner and follower" of Jesus Christ requires us to "go" and "make disciples" of others. Discipleship requires us to move beyond "me-focused" Christianity and into an "others-focused" life.

2. Our workplace is our "nation."

3. Our ability to make disciples at work hinges on three basics…

   a. That we are in fact Christians and that we have a personal relationship with Christ ourselves.

   b. That we go about our work life in a way that earns the respect of our co-workers, superiors, subordinates, suppliers, clients and prospects.

   c. That we become intentional . . . i.e. "on purpose" in our work relationships for the purpose of influencing people toward Christ.

Questions for Discussion

1. Do you feel "the monkey" at your work? How do you respond to it?

2. Christians often live two lives . . . the "Christian" life at church and in those circles, and then the "other" life that includes work and everything else? Where is your "work life" most disconnected from your "church life?"

3. Did you find it difficult to answer the questions in the section called "Be His?" Which question was the hardest to answer? Why?

4. For many, it's a new idea that how we conduct ourselves at our work has a huge impact on our potential influence for Christ. Which of the nine attributes of a great worker is the biggest challenge for you? Why?

5. If you could get just one big thing out of the next six weeks, what would that be?

Notes

"whine time" and then
move on

INTENTIONALITY

Read Pages 30-55 in *About My Father's Business*

Principles and Truths for this week

1. God wants us to be intentional for Him as we go about our jobs.

2. We fail because we forget, we're afraid, and we don't connect with God as we go.

3. The motivation to be a disciple comes from a humble, surrendered heart, and that comes from brokenness and gratitude.

4. God has special blessings for those who follow Him into discipleship.

5. Discipleship is all about relationships.

Memory Verse for Week Two

"But seek first his kingdom and his righteousness, and all these things will be given to you as well."

MATTHEW 6:33

Review

Last week, we got to know the "monkey"…that twinge in our stomachs that hits when we're confronted with a situation at work and we're forced to decide if we're going to respond with faith, or wilt into the woodwork. These moments of truth force us to make decisions. Will we even think about "what Jesus would do?" What impact will our response have on the other person…will it move them closer to Christ or further away? Will I beat my self-righteous chest or can I love and accept my coworker without condoning what they're saying or doing? Hopefully, we've all decided that we want to take the next step ourselves…to become more effective as a Christian witness in our work.

We also talked about "phase I" Christianity, where it's all about me. "I have peace, I have forgiveness, I have purpose, I have a perfect Father who loves and protects me." That's where most of us have stopped and camped out, and it's why so many Christians and the churches they attend are so weak and lifeless.

Jesus calls us to "phase II" Christianity. He wants us to make the move from "me centered" Christianity to the "others centered" life that He modeled for us. Given the direct order to "deny ourselves, take up our cross, and follow Him," we're not given the choice to just stay focused on ourselves. While it's comfortable to be quiet about our faith; to stay passive and to "run and hide" when issues come up at work, that's just not what Jesus told us to do!

We said that three "basics" had to be in place for us to make this transition from "phase I" to "phase II" Christianity. First we must *be His,* and we reviewed the basics of what becoming a Christian involves. Secondly, we said we must *be respected*, and we discovered nine specific things that Scripture says we can do to gain and build the respect of others in our work place.

Then, we learned of our calling to go into the "work nation" and make disciples. Spoken personally by Jesus in all four gospels and in the book of Acts, nothing is clearer than this directive. So, this week we will focus on this third "basic" . . . to *be intentional.*

Two Jobs

Isn't it strange how our jobs never quite satisfy us? Year over year, in survey after survey, we see that between 70 and 90 percent of Americans are dissatisfied with their jobs. Sure we have good days, and even "seasons" when things go well, but most of us feel that we are "underemployed." We know we could handle bigger responsibilities if someone would just trust us and give us the chance. Many of us are burned out in our work, just going through the motions to earn a paycheck.

But what if we got up every day knowing that we were on a mission from God? What if we knew that what we were going to do today mattered, and mattered for all of eternity? What if I knew that I am the only person in the world who can do the job that I am called to do today? Would I feel needed? Significant? Fulfilled?

Well, that's the job you have . . . right now! It is no accident that you are where you are, doing what you are doing in your work. God has assigned you to be his "special agent" to whatever company or organization you're working for.

Being "about my Father's business" means that as I do that "paying job" every day, I am also on a mission for God's invisible kingdom to the people whom I come in contact with in my work "nation." I have my job as supervisor, account executive or associate, but I have my job as "special agent for God" at the same time. Generally, I'm a "secret" agent! But occasionally I have to break out and be public about who I work for and what I'm all about. This "special agent job" is the job of disciple of Jesus Christ. The challenge is put to us in Matthew 6:33. Read the verse and answer these questions.

What does He want us to "seek" first?

What does "and His righteousness" mean?

Where does His "kingdom" exist?

What does "all these things will be given to you as well" refer to?

So, a paraphrase of Matthew 6:33 might say, "Make it your first job (seek first) to be about seeking the hearts of men and women for me, don't forget to seek My righteousness yourself, and I will meet the physical needs of life for you."

The challenge is clear. Christ wants us to pursue the hearts of the men and women that we encounter at work. *He wants us to "be about the Father's business" at work.*

Now, that might have been interpreted a bit differently a few years back. In the traditional view of evangelism in the workplace, we might have thought that being a "special agent for God" meant that you had to . . .

✔ Have a Bible on your desk.

✔ Distribute gospel tracts to coworkers, clients and prospects.

✔ Press everyone you meet to go to church (preferably yours!).

✔ Wear crosses or "Christian jewelry," display Christian symbols in your workspace and on your car.

✔ Start or at least attend a "company" Bible study.

✔ Memorize and be ready to give a presentation of the Gospel, the "four spiritual laws," or something similar.

✔ Be ready to lead a coworker through the "sinner's prayer."

✔ Ask every person in your sphere of influence a "litmus" question such as, "if you died tonight, where would you spend eternity?" If the answer is incorrect, share the gospel and lead them in the sinner's prayer immediately.

✔ Don't rest until everyone you work with has been confronted.

✔ Pray for those who refuse to accept the Gospel.

These are all good things, no doubt. But for many of us, they're just "not me." And we've learned that sometimes, these very things can build walls instead of bridges between us and our unbelieving colleagues.

Here's a different list of things you might see a "special agent for God" doing at work. See which list sounds more like Jesus.

✔ Have an organized prayer life so that God will strengthen you, focus you and lead you in every aspect of your work life, especially in your efforts to influence others for Christ.

✓ Conduct yourself in a manner completely consistent with what God would want . . . a life beyond reproach. Be strong, yet gentle, action oriented, yet patient, tenacious, yet never bowing to pressure or stress.

✓ Do your paying job in an excellent way, so that you are respected and looked up to by everyone.

✓ Love and accept everyone that you come in contact with. This is not tolerance, but genuine, active, demonstrated love and acceptance.

✓ Serve your coworkers, clients, and vendors. Be a humble, consistent servant whose caring turns the heads of everyone.

✓ Know what you believe and why you believe it. Have and be constantly pursuing a knowledge of the Scriptures.

✓ Have a sensitivity for when to speak, and when to just listen.

✓ Be ready, willing and able to "give a defense" of any aspect of your faith, when the situation calls for a defense.

✓ Be a "sought after" resource for Biblical truth and God's answers to life's tough questions.

✓ Be consistently investing in relationships and building trusted friendships, with the intention and purpose of helping people move one step closer to Christ.

✓ Be willing to tell your story, in part or in whole, as a witness to what God has done in your life.

✓ When led by the Spirit, help your "trusted friend" to step over the "line of faith," either by leading him there personally or by bringing him to a pastor or friend who has the tools and experience to lead him into a relationship with Christ.

✓ Follow through with new believers to help them grow.

Sounds like a tall order, huh? We'll get there, but we'll get there one step at a time.

Let's look at two overarching facts; facts that are foundational!

1. *Relationships are everything, because people are the only thing that really count in God's eyes.* That's right. Scripture describes every other thing as temporary . . . as "wood, hay and stubble" that will disappear. Things we so desperately seek, like good looks, social status, owning cool things, being the boss, beautiful memories and pictures from our travels . . . all of this disappears through the years of our lives and at our passing. But people go on forever. Which leads to fact number 2 . . .

2. Everyone will spend eternity somewhere. We've stopped talking much about sin, hell and eternal separation from God. So it shouldn't surprise us that our workmates have less of a felt need to be saved from that fate. But Scripture hasn't changed. We read in Revelation 20:15—

   "If anyone's name was not found written in the book of life, he was thrown into the lake of fire."

   So being about our Father's business is critically important. We have the opportunity and the responsibility to do everything we can to help others avoid this horrible fate.

Becoming "intentional" in our relationships involves having two purposes at the same time. The first purpose is whatever the functional basis of the relationship is to begin with, and the second purpose is to have influence for Christ and to bear fruit. You have a relationship with your boss because he is your boss . . . the receptionist, the shipping manager . . . all these relationships exist because of the functional interaction between your roles at work. So you build and manage these relationships because you have to in order to get your job done. All of this happens all the time at work . . . we hardly ever even think about it.

Take a look at Colossians. 1:10 and fill in below . . .

> *And we pray this in order that you may live a life*
> _____ ____ _____ _____ *and may please*
> *Him in every way: bearing fruit in every* _____
> _____, *growing in the* _____ ____
> _____.

We start as we "live a life worthy of the Lord." This takes us back to those attributes of a worker that gains the respect of his coworkers. Then, we "bear fruit in every good work." This is where we start to see the results of being intentional. And as we see Him produce this "fruit" in our workplace, we will grow in our knowledge of Him and how He works in our lives and in the lives of others as we follow Him.

So, why don't we do it?

Knowing that being a "special agent for God" is so important, why don't we do it? There's nothing all that new or revolutionary here, so why is it so hard for us to be intentional for Christ every day?

Our struggle comes as no surprise to our Lord. Let's look at what the Apostle Paul said about this struggle. Read Romans 7:15 and transcribe it here.

Does that sound like you? It sure sounds like me! I want to exercise but I don't. I hate eating badly, but I do it anyway. Can you relate?

And isn't that the way we are when the "monkey" shows up. We want to be "out there" for Christ . . . we really do! But we "blow it," we "wimp out," or even worse, we "preach them a sermon" that drives them away. There are at least three explanations for why we blow it.

A. *We forget*—we're much less dangerous to Satan when we're busy, and when we're busy, we just forget. "Forget about God, after all He's done for me?" How could we do that? Unfortunately, we do it all the time! And we're not the first generation to be guilty either. In the Old Testament, we see the pattern repeated over and over. God's people turn away from Him… a crisis situation comes and God bails them out… they fall down and worship God in gratitude and wonder… they forget about God and turn away from Him again.

B. *We're afraid*—we think we'll offend someone, or we'll hurt our "reputation" among our colleagues. We don't know what to say. We aren't confident about when we should speak up or keep quiet. We feel woefully inadequate when it comes to knowing Scripture. We may even have a few things we've done or said that we're ashamed of, so we're afraid that people will think our "walk" doesn't match up with our "talk."

C. *We're alone*—we're trying to "do good things for God" without talking to Him about them. We haven't taken the time to pray for ourselves nor for the people whom we work with. We know that we are supposed to be acting as a "special agent for God," but we haven't asked Him what He would have us do, nor gotten His instructions as to how we're supposed to do it.

Your "gratitude bucket"

What will it take to get us "on track" consistently in our daily lives at work? What will it take for us to be intentional . . . to remember and not forget . . . to not be afraid? What will it take to make organized prayer a daily part of our routine?

The answer is *a humble heart* that is *surrendered to the Lord* that realizes that *it's all about God.*

How does one get a humble heart? Well, there's a "high road" and a "low road" to humility. Let me describe them both, and you'll relate.

The "low road" is through brokenness. Many, if not most Christians come to a humble heart through brokenness. We go our own way in life, regardless of how we were raised or what we were taught as children, and at some point it all falls apart. It's a job crisis, a marital crisis, a health crisis, a family crisis, a financial crisis . . . it's some set of circumstances that brings us to our knees. We find that we can't make it on our own, and God is there for us. He delivers us, and we are forever changed because of it. God is real and we know it . . . maybe for the very first time . . . because He showed up in our life & our circumstances and He got us through. He restored us, and we now depend on Him. Our "gratitude bucket" is full and running over.

If the "low road" describes your path to the humble heart, stop right here and write a quick "thank you" note to God. Remind Him of the crisis you were in, how you got into the situation, how He came through for you in that moment, and how His deliverance has changed your life ever since. Don't make Him any promises; just thank Him for giving you a humble heart through brokenness.

Dear God,

Thanks again,

———————————

The "high road" to a humble heart is one of gratitude. Some of us have been raised in Christian homes and in the church. We've never strayed all that far from the "straight and narrow," so it's hard for us to detail the time when we were "broken." Sometimes, that makes it harder for us to see God's hand in our lives. Here's an exercise for you if you can't specify when you were "broken."

There are two columns below; one is titled *Blessings*, the other is titled "*What if*". Take a few minutes and list all of the blessings that you have been given in the first column . . . the people, events, experiences, accomplishments, lessons, and even the material things that you are most thankful for. You might even do this on another sheet so you won't run out of room.

When you've finished your blessings list, then think about what might have been. In the "what if" column, write the opposite of what you wrote in the blessings column. For example, suppose you're grateful for the blessing of good health. In the "what if" column, list how it could have been. You could have kidney problems, requiring weekly dialysis treatments, for example. We will all probably list "salvation" among our blessings, but have we ever thought about what the consequences would have been had He not saved us? Visualize them and write them down.

Spend whatever time it takes to think through and list the opposites of what you have been blessed with and list those outcomes in the second column.

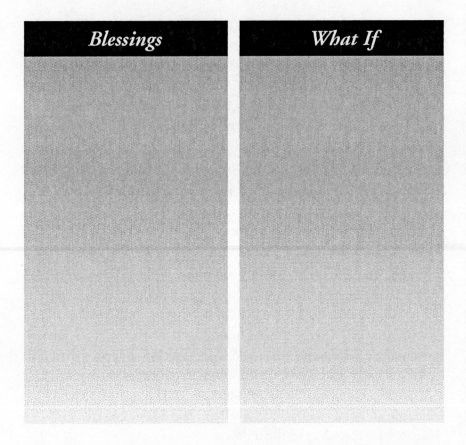

Blessings	What If

Do you see God's hand in your life? Do you see what could have been, were it not for Him? Do you see the blessings and protection that He's provided for you? Aren't you grateful for what He's done and what He keeps on doing for you?

Read James 1:17. Where does every gift come from?

Read Matthew 7:11. Think about how much you enjoy giving "good gifts" to your children. Does God enjoy giving us what we need?

Reflecting upon what God has done for us as well as what He's protected us from fills up our "gratitude bucket." And when it starts to overflow, we find the energy and focus to pray for others, to love and serve them, and to become intentional for Him in every aspect of our lives. We're ready to make our lives a "praise" to Him and, fueled by our overwhelming gratitude, we'll be motivated to be "about our Father's business" every day.

New blessings you'll see

When we take on the second job as "special agent for God," we begin to receive new blessings that we've never had nor experienced. These blessings are just not available to those who stop at "phase I" Christianity and never make the transition to an "others focus." These blessings are described in Scripture, so let's "dig them out" so we'll remember them.

A. *You will have peace*—maybe for the first time in our adult lives, we know that we're doing what Jesus told us to do . . . we're doing His will, and that He is smiling. We can have a peace that is so deep that it can't really be described or understood.

Read John 14:27. What kind of peace can we have?

B. *You will be free from guilt* —all your Christian life, you've felt guilty for not witnessing. When you start to be intentional for Christ and follow the process that we will cover in this study, you'll be free from guilt forever.

Read Galatians 5:1. For what has Christ set us free?

C. *You will be respected*— the body of Christ i.e. the church is connected in a mysterious and supernatural way. When you commit yourself to the life of a disciple, and your words and actions begin to line up behind that calling, you'll gain respect among other believers and among unbelievers as well. Authenticity brings respect, even when people don't believe what you believe.

Read Proverbs 3:3-4. What will we have if we never let love and faithfulness leave us?

D. *You will gain rewards in heaven*—most of us are so busy "doing our thing" here on earth that we never even focus on heaven. We joke about getting another "star in our crown" without ever thinking about what that means. We think "It's going to be so great just to be there, what would I do with a reward beyond that?"

Read Revelation 4:10-11. What will we do with our "rewards" in heaven?

So to summarize, we're called to be active followers of Christ as we do our paying jobs. We have been assigned to be "special agents for God" in our work "nation." We will succeed in our endeavors if we pray, then obey. That way, we're following God's lead in the things we do and the relationships that He leads us into. We will forget, we'll be afraid, and we'll blow it over and over, but He is always there, encouraging us and leading us back into the fray. When we obey His call to live "phase II" of the Christian life, i.e. to become focused on others in addition to ourselves, we get blessings that are extraordinary. We have peace, we're free of guilt, we'll be respected, and we'll have rewards in heaven that we can give back to Him as an offering of gratitude.

Questions for Discussion

1. Think about the people that you have observed attempting to be evangelists and disciple-makers in your work environment. Describe some of the good, the bad and the ugly that you've seen.

2. The idea that we have two jobs is probably a new one. If "disciple making" or being a "special agent for God" were the only job you had in your office, what would you do differently?

3. The movement from a faith that is "I" focused to one that is "others" focused is a huge step. If you took the total amount of energy that you expend on God in an average day, what

percentage of that would be spent on "phase I" or "I" focused things, and what percent would be "phase II" or "others" focused? From a practical point of view, what steps will you take to change those percentages?

4. Which path brought you to the humble, surrendered heart that is ready to "be about our Father's business?" Was it the "low road" of brokenness or the "high road" of gratitude? Explain.

5. As you wrote your "thank you note" to God, or as you listed your blessings and the "what ifs" that could have been, what went through your head? Jot down the thoughts that came to you as you did this exercise and prepare to share them with the group.

 *Notes*

RELATIONSHIPS
ARE THE THING!

Read Pages 56-86 in *About My Father's Business*

Principles and Truths for this week

1. Actively accepting people is a huge part of having influence for Christ at work.

2. Developing your intentionality map will help you focus on people and next steps.

3. Focused, consistent prayer is a necessity if we are to make a difference.

4. Think steps . . . next steps!

Memory Verse for Week Three

"A new command I give you: Love one another. As I have loved you, so you must love one another. By this all men will know that you are my disciples, if you love one another."
        JOHN 13:34-35

Review

We've been getting ourselves ready for the "mission trip" into our "work nation." Last week, we were presented with a job offer—a second job that God wants us to do while we do our paying job. He wants us to be His "Special agents," living every work day in touch with Him so that we will . . .

✓ "Seek His kingdom" . . . i.e. be intentional about winning the hearts of men for Him.

✓ "Seek His righteousness" in our own lives by having an intimate, growing, personal relationship with God.

✓ Be the kind of person and employee that people at his workplace will respect and look up to.

The motivation to do this job—to be intentional about your Father's business—will come from gratitude. Whether it's gratitude for what Christ did for you at the cross, gratitude for His deliverance from your brokenness, or gratitude for what He's blessed you with, your long term source of sustained motivation to live the "phase II," "others focused" Christian life is *gratitude*.

Building Your Intentionality Map

Following the instructions on pages 58 through 69 of *About My Father's Business*, create your Intentionality Map, or IMAP. (See page 95 of this guide for an IMAP.)

The IMAP is intended to be a starting point for becoming intentional for Christ in your work relationships. It's a "first draft" snapshot of the people that God has put on your "radar screen" from your work "nation." Over the coming weeks, we'll look at aspects of each of the five spiritual profiles and discuss things we can do to help everyone in our sphere of influence take their next step.

Relationships and Your Sphere of Influence

If we believe that God is omniscient (knows everything) and omnipotent (has unlimited power), then it is not an accident that you work where you work. You may only be there for a season, but you can be sure that you are there for a reason! And the people that you work with are a big part of that reason. God has some work for you to do in the lives of the people you work with, and He's going to do some work in you while you're at it.

Read John 13:34-35 (*our memory verse for the week*)

What's the command from our "Boss"?

If our job is to love others the way that He loves us, just how *does* He love us?

Who will know that we're His disciples ("special agents")?

"Love" is such a popular word these days, yet it's a word that few people can accurately define and even fewer put any effort to. Outside our closest friends and family, love is a noun rather than a verb.

We want to turn "love" into a verb when it comes to the people on our IMAP, and we're going to start with two simple steps. If we will train and motivate ourselves to do these two things, we will start a revolution in the hearts of these people . . . a revolution that might just lead to an overthrow of the current regime (selfishness and sin) and the coronation of a new regime . . . Salvation and Righteousness!

Acceptance

Modern day Christians are not known for their acceptance of people . . . we're much more identified with judging people. Deserved or not, we're perceived to be "down on" people who aren't like us. Christians reject abortion, divorce, homosexuality, drugs, premarital sex, living together before marriage, pornography, and any religion other than ours. But we must learn to accept and communicate our acceptance of people who have done or are currently doing these things.

Recognize that this is a list of *decisions* people have made . . . not kinds of people that we reject. We have to discipline ourselves to accept people who have made these decisions (and many others neither we nor Scripture would agree with).

When you listed your "workmates" on your IMAP, did you leave someone off because you just don't like them? Or you don't respect them because of their involvement in some of the things listed above? Keep those names at the top of your mind . . . we'll come back to them in just a minute.

First, let's read the story of Zacchaeus in Luke 19:1-10

Which did Jesus communicate first . . . love or acceptance? (vs. 5)

What change in behavior did Jesus require of Zacchaeus before he demonstrated His acceptance and went to his house to visit?

What changes in his behavior did Zacchaeus choose to make after Jesus demonstrated His acceptance?

Acceptance is a powerful, powerful thing! We all consciously and subconsciously gravitate *toward* people and environments where we are *accepted*, and we gravitate *away* from environments of *rejection*.

Think for a few minutes about people on your IMAP that you have "issues" with. This may include the names you passed over before and chose not to put on your IMAP. List them below in column A. Then jot down in column B just one word that describes the issue. "Hot head," "Smart alec," "Critical," "Know it all," "Muslim," "Alternative," "Adulterer," "Pothead," "Punk," "Show off" . . . these might be some of the descriptive words that come to mind. Now in column C, jot down one word that describes how you could respond to that person the next time you encounter them. "Smile," "Eye contact," "Hug," "Ask about her mother," "Accept," or just the word "Pray." How would Jesus respond to this person? Remember that you're on a mission from God, and your job is to communicate acceptance . . . what do you do?

Issue Person	*The Issue*	*Your new "acceptance" response*

You see, our natural tendency is to hang out with people who are like us. It's the old "birds of a feather" concept. Problem is, it's not Biblical and it's not what Jesus taught or modeled. He was a "friend of sinners," not to mention tax collectors, lepers and other societal outcasts. He entered into relationships with those people in order to have influence with them and to accomplish His Father's purpose. We must go and do the same.

Prayer

What greater act of love is there than to think of the name of a coworker and to call out that name to the Creator of the universe? When we start to realize that God has put our coworkers into our lives for some purpose, then we know that we have to pray for them if we are to fulfill it. We will fail miserably if we try to do it on our own or make it up as we go.

Through prayer, God will direct the steps of your relationships with people that you are attempting to influence for Him. Praying for them will change your outlook toward them. It may even make it easier for you to love them when they are radically different from you. More importantly, prayer can change them, their environment, and the way they see you, God, life, their past and the future. Remember, it's God who is at work here, to "will and to work for His purposes." We're just "special agents," doing our jobs which includes a lot of praying.

Our goal with people who are apathetic toward spiritual things is to spark an interest . . . to inspire them to begin a search! We can best do that by:

✓ Living out our faith consistently before them. That means loving, serving, and not judging.

✓ Accepting them just as they are and communicating our acceptance.

✓ Praying for them consistently and purposefully. For those in column A, our prayer is that God would light that spark of interest in Him.

✓ Listening and paying attention to them, so that we can learn what they really believe. Everyone believes in something… it's our job to gracefully and patiently find out what that is for the people on our IMAP.

Remember, we treat everyone we meet and everyone in our sphere of influence as if they were apathetic until we learn otherwise.

 ## Questions for Discussion

1. As you prayerfully listed the names of the people in your work "nation" on your IMAP, what was your biggest struggle?

2. Contrast the word "acceptance" with the word "tolerance."

3. Many of us have experienced "divine appointments," where we have prayed for someone, gotten some unction to do something, done it, and then seen some incredible result that could only have come from God's involvement. Jot down enough of one of those stories that you can share it with the group.

4. How do we communicate acceptance to the person who is involved in "sin" and things we don't condone, without communicating our acceptance for their behavior?

5. How long should we "stay in the game" with people on our IMAP? How do we decide to add someone, and how do we decide to take someone off?

   *Note- Question 5 will get a lot of attention. It relates to when you remove someone from your IMAP. The answer is "when God allows you to". If someone moves out of your sphere of influence (leaves town, leaves the company, etc) you will sometimes feel a peace about taking them off your list. But God may want you to continue to pray for that person and maybe even stay in touch. God is the one who leads you to put people on your list, and He's the only one who frees you to take them off.

Notes

GOING ON THE JOURNEY WITH THEM!

Read Pages 87-111 in *About My Father's Business*

Principles and Truths for this week

1. People who are "beginning to search" are interested in spiritual things. They are active in their search for Truth. They may be "seeking," or they may think that they have found the truth, but it's not in Jesus Christ.

2. We face our need for God when there is disruption in our lives.

3. Our goal as "special agents for God" is to live and relate in such a way that we earn a position of respect and influence in the lives of those "seekers," so that when "disruption" happens, we'll be positioned to point them to Christ.

4. Telling your own story can be a powerful tool in pointing a seeker to Christ.

Memory Verse for Week Four

"Then you will know the truth, and the truth will set you free."
JOHN 8:32

Review

Our lives are defined by relationships—with God, with our parents, our children, with our spouses, with our workmates. Becoming intentional in our work relationships starts with identifying people in our sphere of influence and putting their names on our "Intentionality Map." Then, we are to pray for them and make an effort to accept them, just as they are, just as Jesus accepts us!

Hope Rises from Movement!

As a kid, my favorite week of the year was vacation. Even more than Christmas, I loved it when my dad would start to load stuff in the car. Mom had made cookies and bought potato chips for the long ride. There was incredible excitement in the air! We're getting ready to *go*!

That's the excitement that comes when someone you've invested in starts to show an interest in spiritual things. Just like those childhood vacations, we have no idea where we're going, how long it's going to take, nor what roads we're going to travel on the way. But there's excitement when we're going on a trip. And when Dad is driving, we can relax and enjoy the ride because He knows the way. Same here!

When that spark gets ignited in someone, you can be sure that God is involved. Augustine said "There's a God-shaped hole in every man's heart."

God made us that way. He won't force us to love Him. He won't even force us to look for Him, but He's there, hoping that we'll pursue Him of our own free will. Scripture tells us that's part of why God created us and put us in "nations" all over the world.

> *"God did this so that men would seek him and perhaps reach out for him and find him, though he is not far from each one of us." ACTS 17:27*

We want to help those who are beginning to search to find Truth, but we can't forget a couple of important facts. Read Titus 2:10, and pay particular attention to the last part of the verse.

What character quality are believers encouraged to exhibit?

He wants us to show we can be fully _____

Why?

Remember, statistics show that over 80% of adults who come to Christ do so through the influence of a *trusted friend!*

How do we build that trust? By telling the truth, by saying what we're going to do and then doing it, and by being "over the top" in being honest, in every detail of our lives.

Becoming a trusted friend with someone that we don't know very well also involves some diplomacy. We have to become "safe" to them. They have to know they can share their opinions (including their doubts and "heretical" questions) with us. We have to earn the right to talk about personal things. Importantly, we must then have the patience to wait until there is an interest—a need to know—and that usually comes after some disruption event.

How can we earn the right to be trusted in such a sensitive area as faith? Matthew 10:16 says, "I am sending you out like sheep among wolves. Therefore be as shrewd as snakes and as innocent as doves."

The Greek word used here for "shrewd" means ""thoughtful" or "discreet." God is urging us to pray . . . to contemplate with Him what the best "next step" for your friend might be. God wants to help you respond as Jesus would. When He sent us into the work "nation," He made a huge promise that we can depend on—that He "will always be with us."

James gives us more instruction on what we're to do as we go on this journey with our work mate. Read James 1:19-20.

He tells us to be _____ to listen.

"Quick" implies eager. When others are expressing their opinions and beliefs, are we eagerly listening to what they're really saying, or are we tolerating them . . . waiting until it's our turn, so we can tell them what WE believe? That's a huge lesson—don't miss it!

We're to be _____ to speak.

Could it be that His advice to be "slow to speak" is so He can have time to guide us . . . to show us how to be thoughtful and discreet when we do finally respond? When we say things we wish we hadn't said, isn't it usually because we didn't take time to think about what we said, or how it might be received?

We're to be _____ to anger, "for man's anger does not bring about the righteous life that God desires."

This last phrase tells us that we're not going to accomplish anything in our own lives nor in the lives of the people we're trying to influence by allowing ourselves to get angry.

Who hasn't had a heated discussion about religion? It's probably the most volatile subject that we can talk about. Yet, how many times have you seen someone emerge from one of those "discussions" (arguments!) saying "Oh yeah, you know . . . you're right! I've changed my mind today based on what you said!" Never.

"Going on the journey with them" means that we "keep our cool" and avoid heated discussions and "hot spot" topics. We thoughtfully and discreetly point them to Truth, and we do it under God's direction (which is usually a lot slower than we'd like!)

As one wise teacher puts it, "Do you want to make a point or build a bridge?" Making a point can get you kicked off the journey; building bridges makes you a valuable traveling companion.

Dialogue vs. Discussion

Think about the word *discussion*. When we "dis" something, we "*dis*card" it, or we "*dis*ect" things in the biology lab. The last part of the word "discussion" comes from the same root as the word "percussion." So when we "discuss" something, we're "hitting it back and forth."

Now, contrast that with the word *dialogue*. "Di" means "multiple" and "logue" means "truth" . . . dialogue is when two are seeking truth together.

You can't create an environment that fosters dialogue if you know it all! Read the caution given to us in 1 Cor. 8:1-2.

Knowledge _____ ____, but love _____ _____.

What does verse 2 say about humility?

If we are "known by God," do we have any pressure to "know it all?" Why or why not?

When we're going on the journey with someone, we're seeking truth together. Sometimes, we'll get to lead . . . telling our story, suggesting ideas, books to read, CDs to listen to, etc. But sometimes, they'll be leading . . . taking the "rabbit trail" off into all kinds of theologies . . . reading and considering things that you know are wrong. That's when we have to listen and pray, love and accept, and wait for the opportunity to lead them back to the path that will lead to Truth. Sometimes, you may even have to read or listen to something that you know is not true in order to help your friend see the problem. Ask God to protect you and give you His insight as you defend your faith against the deception of the evil one.

Read Col. 4:5-6

God instructs us to be _____. Sometimes that means holding back on showing that we're right!

What are our conversations to be full of?

If we're wise in our conversations, and full of grace, then we'll know how to answer _____.

Meeting People Where They Are

The apostle Paul was an incredible evangelist for Jesus Christ. Read 1 Cor. 9:19-23 below . . .

> *"Though I am free and belong to no man, I make myself a slave to everyone, to win as many as possible. To the Jews I became like a Jew, to win the Jews. To those under the law I became like one under the law (though I myself am not under the law), so as to win those under the law. To those not having the law I became like one not having the law (though I am not free from God's law but am under Christ's law), so as to win those not having the law. To the weak I became weak, to win the weak. I have become all things to all men so that by all possible means I might save some. I do all this for the sake of the gospel, that I may share in its blessings."*

So is Paul telling us to become "chameleons" . . . to be dishonest?

Ingenuine?

Not at all. He's just saying "go on the journey with them"—meet them where they are, just as Jesus accepted you and met you right where you were!

The Journey Ends in Only One Place

With all of this wisdom about how to relate to the "seeker" in our workplace, never get confused about the final destination . . . and that is faith in Jesus Christ alone. Read the words of Jesus in John 14:6 and then read Acts 4:12.

If we and our coworkers are to find our way to the Father, then how will we get there?

In whom is salvation exclusively found? _____

_____

Your Story

Earlier in this study, we reflected on four very specific personal questions.

1. What was your life like before you trusted Christ?

2. What were the circumstances that drove you to need Christ in your life?

3. What happened in the 24 hours surrounding your committing your life to Christ?

4. What has your life been like since you became a Christian?

(We've learned this pattern for telling our story by reading how Paul told his story to King Agrippa in Acts 26:2-22. Read those verses and you'll clearly see Paul answer these four questions as he tells his story.)

Telling your story may be the most powerful and effective thing you can do to inspire a person who is seeking truth to look closely at Jesus Christ. Why? Here are a few good reasons:

1. No one can argue with your story. What happened to you happened to you! It's impossible for someone to disprove your own personal experience.

2. The invisible meets the visible. While God is invisible, you're not. When you tell the story of how the invisible God made visible changes in *you personally* and the "seeker" has seen substance of that in how you live, that's powerful evidence that the God you're describing is real.

3. No training required. Everyone who has encountered Jesus Christ has a story. We can *all* tell our story . . . we simply need the sensitivity to know the right time and the courage to act.

Scripture tells the story of Jesus healing a man who had been blind from birth (John 9:1-25). After being pounded with all kinds of questions about Jesus (questions the man didn't know the answers to) he shared one irrefutable truth:

"One thing I do know; I was blind but now I see."

We will never know all the answers, but we do know our own story. Being willing to take the risk and tell it may be the "billboard" your workmate needs to see to make that final turn toward the destination . . . a relationship with Christ.

If you've never done it before . . . if you need to refresh your memory, or if you just need to practice, write your story now and ask God to give you an opportunity to tell it to someone this week.

 ## Questions for Discussion

1. What do you think about the idea that "disruption" is the catalyst that starts our movement toward God?

2. Think of two work situations where you saw the absolute truth either violated or upheld. What impact did these situations have on your thinking and belief system?

3. How do you know when to abandon the journey—to "dust off your sandals" and move on? What does moving on look like?

4. We can actively demonstrate love to those in our sphere of influence by sharing our knowledge, our network, and by showing compassion. What makes this a good "investment?"

5. Think back to the person who was most influential in your coming to Christ. Did he/she accept you? Love you? Pray for you? Think about their role in your "disruption event" and how God used them to bring you to Himself. What lessons can you learn and apply to your relationships with "seekers" or people who are in "disruption?"

Notes

TAKING THEM ON A JOURNEY WITH YOU!

Read Pages 112-143 in *About My Father's Business*

Principles and Truths for this week

1. Believing is a starting point, not an end for the Christian.

2. Mediocrity is disgusting to the Lord . . . He wants our whole heart.

3. Our faith can be "choked" by distractions and things we put before our "first love."

4. We are to "spur one another on," and we can best do that by inviting others to join us as we pursue God ourselves.

Memory Verse for Week Five

"And let us consider how we may spur one another on toward love and good deeds."   HEBREWS 10:24

Review

Last week, we focused on the non-believers in our sphere of influence who are actively seeking spiritual answers. We learned that becoming a "trusted friend" is critical, and how we have to demonstrate our genuine acceptance of people who are not like us and don't believe what we believe. We were reminded about the need to listen more than we talk and our need for patience. We have to become intentional "pray-ers," praying for the people we work with. We were warned about arguments and "discussions" of religion, and how anger can get a foothold and cause us to blow good opportunities. Finally, we went back to our own story . . . the story of how we came to Christ and the importance of having the willingness and the ability to tell it at the right time. This week, we'll focus on the confessing Christian, and our opportunity to help him take his next step.

"Oh, sure. I believe."

Our country is full of Christians, isn't it? All the surveys say it is. Over 60% say they're Christians and almost everyone says they believe in God. (Isn't that almost the same thing?)

"I go to church sometimes." "I'm a member at Saint Marks." "Oh sure, I believe."

C.S. Lewis compared passive and active Christianity to the Atlantic Ocean and a map of the Atlantic Ocean. Lots of people have seen the ocean. They know it's real . . . they've experienced it! They've viewed its expanse and its power with awe! But that's as far as they've gone.

They have only walked on the beach.

If we want to *go somewhere* on that ocean, we need a map. A map gives us the benefit of the experience of thousands of people who have traveled the Atlantic before us. "As long as you are content with walks on the beach, your own glimpses are far more fun than looking at a map. But the map is going to be more use than the walks on the beach if you want to get to America," said Lewis.

We need both the ocean and the map—belief in Christ and a journey to join Him on! We need the awe of God, particularly of the love that He has for us. But we also need to respond to that love . . . to go somewhere with it, and for that we need a map (and a few other things too, but we'll come to those in a minute).

The Maze of Mediocrity

Jesus warned us about "beach walking." He knew that our "awe of the ocean" could fade as we became immersed in life. Read Luke 8:14.

What "chokes" the faith of believers?

When and where does it happen?

When a plant fails to mature, what are the consequences?

Jesus also knew that we would try to mature . . . to earn His approval by creating "maps" that would tell people how to be "holy." Jesus personally saw and experienced this kind of "religiosity" as He saw the Pharisees reduce God to an impossible formula of rules and laws. Because we can't sustain an emotional passion for God AND because we can't measure up to the performance requirements of following the "map," we give up on both and fall into mediocrity . . . with predictable results. Read Matthew 5:13.

Who did Jesus call "the salt of the earth?"

What is salt that has lost its saltiness?

What happens to salt when it loses its saltiness?

Our Christian faith can become useless, "thrown out" (implying that it's put someplace where it's not in the way) and "trampled on by men" (meaning it's not valuable enough to use, protect or defend). Does that describe the faith of anyone you know?

In Revelation 3:15-16, He graphically describes His reaction to Christians who "lose their first love" and become "lukewarm."

How does He know that we're neither "hot nor cold?"

How does mediocrity or being "lukewarm" about Jesus make God feel?

Why is God's reaction to mediocrity so strong?

Remember, the opposite of love isn't hate . . . it's apathy! God isn't surprised by our love response to Him, nor is He shocked when people reject Him. That's an exercise of the free will that God gave us. It's the "inbetweeners" that make him sick!

What's Our Assignment?

Just as with "apathetics" and with those who are beginning to search, we're charged with loving and serving these "confessing Christians." We're often tempted to judge "nominal" Christians because they don't do the things we do. And as we said earlier, people are attracted to people who accept them, but avoid those who judge and reject them. Read Romans 14:3.

What are we told *not to do* when fellow believers don't subscribe to the same religious practices that we do?

What has God done for both?

Keeping our mouths shut about "non-essential" elements of Christian doctrine helps build bridges with fellow believers!

Scripture goes on to give us three very specific instructions or assignments regarding relationships with "confessing Christians." Read Hebrews 10: 23-25.

The three assignments are . . .

1. . . ."hold _____ to the hope we profess". We
   keep on "living out loud" a life that is attractive to all who
   know us.

2. . . . "consider how we may _____ ____ _____on
   toward love and good deeds." It's our job to figure out how to
   encourage other Christians toward love for God, and toward
   good deeds for people.

3. . . . "not give up _____ _____." We're challenged
   to "stay in the game" with other Christians. We can't
   encourage other Christians if we aren't connected to them in
   on-going relationships.

"Follow Me" Means You

Jesus went places and took His disciples with Him almost
everywhere He went. As they followed along, often simply observing
. . . sometimes participating . . . sometimes asking questions, their
faith matured. Did they have their setbacks? Sure they did. But all
but one spent their lives spreading the Gospel after Jesus was no
longer physically present and most died as martyrs as a result.

There are thousands of workplace Bible studies in almost every
city. Find one and invite your "confessing Christian" friend to go with
you. If you can't find one, ask him to join you in starting one. There's
almost nothing better to inspire a passive Christian to become active
than regular Bible study with trusted friends. It is so easy to tell
someone about a study . . . to say "you should go." But it's a hundred
times more effective to say "go with me" and take them.

Invite your Christian friends to get involved with you in your ministry activities. Don't just tell them about the short term mission trip, sign up to go and invite them to go with you. You can also invite them into your small group . . . "as you go," they can follow you there. So much of the anxiety of new and challenging environments is reduced when one can go with their trusted friend.

Bring them to special events at your church, even if you know they come from a different denominational tradition. Explain that you're not "proselytizing" . . . you just want to share a particular sermon, service, performance or speaker with them.

Sometimes, their faith can be ignited by involvement in a musical or drama production. Volunteer for things that are of genuine interest to you and or your friend. Thousands have gotten involved in "Habitat for Humanity" and similar projects. There are camping ministries, Young Life and Student Venture ministries for high schoolers, and all kinds of opportunities to get involved with college students and internationals. If you and your workmate love to hike, look for opportunities to join in with youth groups who are heading to the trails.

Pray and Obey

Remember, the process is the same: pray for your "confessing Christian" coworkers; develop relationships with them; love and serve them. Ask God for instructions as to how He would have you "spur them on," then obey whatever He tells you to do. Don't put pressure on them, and don't put pressure on yourself. Pray and obey. That's it . . . pray and obey.

When you ask God to show you projects that you can connect your "C" friends to, don't be surprised when He does. Connecting them to a "cause" can be catalytic to their faith, launching them into "growth mode" and moving them from Phase I to Phase II… from passive to active, from mediocrity to excellence. And along the way, you'll get the blessing of knowing God used you—especially you—to create another disciple!

Questions for Discussion

1. How do you identify the "chosen frozen" in your workplace?

2. What kinds of things "choke out" our faith at work? What can we do to keep it vibrant and growing?

3. We often relate "spurring one another on" to "encouraging" someone. How can we "build courage into" someone who has been shy and retreating about their faith in Jesus Christ?

4. What has been your biggest challenge in becoming more active and "others focused" in your faith?

FROM "IT"
TO "HIM"

Read Pages 144-154 in *About My Father's Business*

Principles and Truths for this week

1. Many people are confused, thinking that Christianity is an "it" . . . i.e. something you do or a set of principles.

2. "Going pubic" or telling others about your faith is a key first step in becoming a "developing disciple."

3. Learning and applying God's Word is a "must do" for growth in your faith.

4. Prayer brings God into current reality for us and allows us to have an interactive relationship with Him.

5. Connecting with other Christians fuels our growth through encouragement and accountability.

Memory Verse for Week Six

So then, just as you received Christ Jesus as Lord, continue to live in him, rooted and built up in him, strengthened in the faith as you were taught, and overflowing with thankfulness.
COL. 2: 6-7

Review

Last week, we discussed the "confessing Christians" in our lives . . . those who say they believe but aren't active in pursuing a more intense relationship with God. We saw that their faith and fate may be secure (i.e. they are still "salt") but they are of no use to God. And that's a pretty significant blow when we know that true meaning and fulfillment in life comes from being used of Him in the lives of others. We were also reminded of the passion with which God views mediocrity when we were reminded of His plans to "spew out of His mouth" those who have lost their first love and become lukewarm. We were warned that all kinds of things can distract us from our faith and can choke out our ability to grow and mature. We were also cautioned about passing judgment on other Christians because they are in a different place or have different religious practices from us. Instead, we were encouraged to connect with confessing Christians and invite them to go with us into a deeper relationship with Christ.

Getting Personal

Having religion is easy. It's something you do, and everyone can learn to do it. Anyone can learn the "church speak." We can become master "church attenders" by knowing when to stand up, sit down, kneel, and read the right paragraph out loud.

Many confessing Christians de-personalize faith . . . "I believe in *it*" they say. It's just so much harder to refer to "Him." We can talk about church or our set of beliefs as an inanimate "it." But we struggle to refer to "Him" because that's a transition from a thing to a person, and that's the defining difference of Christianity.

In fact, it's really easier in our culture to have a religion than to not have one. The questions are easier to answer . . . "Oh yes, I'm Catholic" or "I'm Jewish" or "I'm Christian" . . . all of those labels roll off the tongue pretty easily.

But Christianity isn't a label . . . it's not even something you do. It's something that you are and it's derived from Someone you know. When our faith is mature, it's definitional... our "real time," interactive relationship with the living God becomes the center of our lives every day. He holds major "mindshare," and our every thought and action is touched by that interactive relationship. He prompts us to pray, He causes us to wince in our souls when we are insensitive or mean to someone. He brings a tear to our eye when we see His hand in a situation or a sunset that reminds us of how much He loves us. When we look for Him, we'll see that He's there all the time, making Himself known in all kinds of ways, big and small.

The path to this meaningful, daily, personal relationship with Christ begins when we first truly believe in Him. Look at Romans 10:9.

Our first instruction is to _____ "Jesus is Lord,"

But we're also reminded that we must _____ that God raised him from the dead, you will be saved.

There are no "magic words" that take us to heaven. Saying the words AND believing in our hearts will.

And so it is, and so it stays with so many of our fellow Christians. They cheat themselves out of so much by stopping with their salvation and failing to develop in their relationship with their Heavenly Father.

"Going Public"

Step one in becoming a developing disciple is to let people know that you are one. That can be a huge challenge for Christians . . . especially new believers and especially new adult believers. It's the "what will people think" syndrome. We can rock along in our "chosen frozen" state and nobody is going to notice us, nor ask us any questions. But when we start talking openly about Jesus Christ, and the difference He makes in our lives, attention is going to be drawn to us and we're going to have to either "go public" or run and hide. Jesus anticipated this and gave us a clear picture of the consequences of the decisions we make in those "moments of truth." Read Matthew 10:32-33 and answer these questions.

What does Jesus promise to do for those who acknowledge Him before men?

What are the consequences of "disowning" Him before men?

The first "hurdle" we have to get over in moving from "confessing Christian" to "developing disciple" is to let others know that we are committed to living our lives for Jesus Christ.

So What Is a Developing Disciple?

From our memory verse, Col. 2: 6-7, we see an order for developing as a disciple. Jot down what you think is meant by each word set . . .

First . . . "received Jesus Christ"—

Second . . . "continue to live in Him"—

Third . . . "rooted and built up in Him"—

Fourth . . . "strengthened in your faith as you were taught"—

Fifth . . . "overflowing with thankfulness"—

The "roots" of our faith are found in the Bible. That's where we learn about God, the ways of God and the "roadmap" for our lives, Jesus Christ. So we can't become developing disciples without getting "rooted" in God's Word.

Anyone can pick up a Bible, read it and grow. Millions do it every day. But there is so much more that's gained by studying the Bible with a group, sharing insights and experiences, and allowing the Spirit to teach. In addition, there are thousands of books that record the insights of brilliant people who have spent their whole lives translating, studying and interpreting the Scriptures. We have such leverage to get the benefit of lifetimes of learning, all within our grasp . . . if we will only commit the time, and read.

But Bible knowledge, in and of itself, doesn't make one a developing disciple. Jesus pointed this out to the religious leaders of His day in John 5:37-40. Read those verses now and answer the questions below.

What's the difference between "studying the Scriptures" and having the Word "dwell in you?"

We can't "have life" by simply studying the Scriptures . . . we must _____ to have life.

Developing disciples distill the principles taught in Scripture and apply them to their everyday lives. But they're only able to effectively do that as they pray and ask God to teach them.

To Pray or Not to Pray

To grow up "in Him" says that we grow up in His image. We can read the words of Jesus in the Bible... we can even get a mental picture of how Jesus responded in different situations that might look the ones we face. But if we are going to "have life and have it to the full," we are going to have to "come to Him," early and often. The developing disciple is in constant dialogue with God, praying for Himself and for others, praying for understanding, for patience, for wisdom, even praying that God will give him enough faith to believe that his prayers are going somewhere.

Read Eph. 6:18 and respond to these questions:

Does he really mean to pray "on all occasions?"

What are some of the "kinds" of prayers we can make?

To "always keep on praying" means nonstop . . . is that reasonable?

Why do you think we are reminded to "be alert"?

To become learners and followers of Christ, we must always be alert for the application of Scripture to the situation that we're in, or to the decision that we're facing. God is alive and interactive. He's responsive to our prayers. He wants us to learn. And most of all, He wants us to emulate His beloved Son in every aspect of our lives. So God, through the Holy Spirit, is actively involved in our development. He prompts, He challenges, He teaches, He flashes questions into our heads. Jesus explained this as part of the job of the "Counselor" in John 14:26. Read that verse and answer below.

In whose name will the "Counselor" be sent?

What will the "Counselor" teach us?

What will the "Counselor" remind us of?

It's easier for God to remind us of things Jesus said when we've heard them at least once before. We can only hear them the first time by reading and remembering Scripture.

Isn't it cool that God promises to be involved in our development, and all that He asks is that we be involved first?

Fellowship—THE Source of Accountability and Encouragement

We all do better when someone is watching. Fellowship brings accountability, and when developing disciples meet together there is a natural accountability that happens. Notice what has happened through the first five weeks of this study . . . people have shown up; they've studied their Bibles, they've discussed different ideas and strategies for becoming more like Jesus. Would that have happened to the same degree if you had taken this study on "all by your lonesome?" Not likely. Take a look at Eph. 4:15-16 and answer below.

What is the "whole body?"

What is God's role in the development of "the body" and the disciples who make up "the body?"

Describe how the word "synergy" applies to these verses.

Along with accountability, being connected ("in fellowship") with other disciples gives us a source of encouragement. We're affirmed when we see others trying to do the same thing we're trying to do. Hearing of their successes AND of their setbacks can give us the courage to keep on keeping on! Read 1 Thess. 5:11—

> *"Therefore encourage one another and build each other up, just as in fact you are doing."*

Look at the "Ds" on your IMAP and ask God to show you the name of the person He would have you encourage today with a call or email. Do it now, and write the name of the person below.

Developing Disciples and "Outsiders"

When we make the decision to follow Christ, I mean, really follow Christ, we're embarking on a new life of adventure. All the things we've been talking about are pretty "out there" . . . reading and memorizing Scripture, praying all the time, (and about everything) . . . meeting with other Christians to challenge and encourage them. But nothing is as scary as beginning to think about sharing our faith with "outsiders." It's a harrowing thought for many of us . . . the prospect that we might actually tell our own personal story or, scarier still, lead someone to Christ.

All of these things take courage and faith—sometimes what seems like blind faith. Let's close this week by reading the words of the Old Testament prophet Isaiah, from Isaiah 42:16—

> *I will lead the blind by ways they have not known,*
> *along unfamiliar paths I will guide them; I will turn*
> *the darkness into light before them and make the*
> *rough places smooth. These are the things I will do;*
> *I will not forsake them.*

Isn't it comforting to know that while we're struggling to know what we're to do, how to share, when to speak up and when to stay silent . . . that the God of the universe is quietly leading the "outsiders" in our lives down a path that leads to Him. Sure, they can remain in the "opt out" mode and reject Him, but that's not our responsibility. We're to become mature disciples ourselves as we love and accept them. Then, we're to pray and obey what He urges us to do. We rest, knowing that God is at work, drawing our colleagues toward Himself, and that it is His will for all to come to know Him.

Questions for Discussion

1. Name some of the visible, "public" activities that "developing disciples" will be found being involved in.

2. Thinking back to the time when you crossed over the "line of faith" and became a Christian, who was the most influential person involved in your decision? What did they do that stands out in your memory today as most significant?

3. Describe a "lie" that the enemy has used to keep you from growing in your faith. What was the fear that his lie paralyzed you with? What have you done (or what must you do) to break free from that fear and get on with being "about our Father's business"?

THE EXCELLING CHRISTIAN. . . AT WORK

Read Pages 155-170 in *About My Father's Business*

Principles and Truths for this week

1. The distinguishing characteristic of an "excelling Christian" is their intentionality for seeing others move one step closer to Christ.

2. We are partners with God in our efforts to work in the lives of people.

3. Teaming up with another Christian gives us strength, encouragement, prayer coverage and access to other brains and other perspectives.

4. We must be careful because the enemy is active in our work place and is looking for ways to deceive and work against us.

Memory Verse for Week Seven

"Have I not commanded you? Be strong and courageous. Do not be terrified; do not be discouraged, for the Lord your God will be with you wherever you go."
JOSHUA 1:9

Review

Developing disciples are fun people to be around, because they love God and they're excited about what He's doing in their lives. They are public about their faith, participating in small groups or other "growth" activities. They have "grown up" in their faith to the point that they know how to pray and how to spot God's hand in their circumstances. Disciples have learned enough Scripture to have a pretty clear picture of the ways of God, a good understanding of the principles of God and a personal vision of what Jesus is like. Most importantly, they have a good grasp of what Jesus would have them do in most situations, and by and large, they try to do it.

Developing disciples have learned the value of connecting with other believers. They know that the accountability and encouragement they get from insiders will propel them to become intentional toward "outsiders." And that intentionality is what moves a "D" to an "E" . . . an excelling Christian!

Reaching Out

The final, and in many cases, the highest hurdle we have to clear in our walk with Christ is sharing our faith with others. As we said earlier, we've mistakenly defined "evangelism" or "sharing our faith" as an event . . . when it's really a process. Since God is responsible for the outcome, the question is really about whether we will have the courage to try . . . to focus on others and become *intentional* in our prayers and relationships. Virtually everything we do in a relationship can have a spiritual motive and when it does, we are "on task" of glorifying God in our lives. When we *intentionally* love, *intentionally* serve, *intentionally* accept, *intentionally* forgive, *intentionally* invite, *intentionally* pray for a person at work, with the motive (or intention) of obeying and pleasing God, then we are about our Father's business in that activity. It's that broad, and that simple! Becoming an "excelling E" means that you've accepted the job of pursuing the hearts of men and women for Christ, not just enjoying the benefits of Christianity yourself.

Joining Forces

When we take the first step and declare our intention to God, He often gives us help. That help usually comes through another "excelling Christian" who cares for others just like you do.

There is nothing quite like having a friendship with another "excelling Christian" where working together to make a difference for Christ is central to the relationship. Read 1 Cor. 3:5-9, where Paul describes his "partnership" with Apollos.

What binds Paul and Apollos together? (*verse 8*)

How will each be rewarded?

With whom are we "fellow workers"?

So our partnership isn't just with other excelling Christians, it's also with God Himself. Isn't it awesome to know that we are working in partnership *with* God . . . not just trying to do something good *for* God! We are united with Christ on our "mission from God."

Read Philip. 2:1-2

God wants us to be _____minded.

God wants us to have the _____ love.

God wants us to be one in spirit and _____.

Every challenge in life is easier to face when we have partners. Yes, Jesus is always with us, but it gives us courage to step out when we know other people are going with us. Read Eccl. 4: 9-12 and fill in your answers below.

What are four reasons that it's better to have "partners" in your workplace ministry?

  1.

2.

3.

4.

Because we are working in partnership with God, we can trust that He will meet all our needs. Sometimes we find ourselves in a job or an organization where we feel like we're the only Christian in the place. But we must be patient and alert. God rarely sends us out alone, and in time, we'll likely find other Christians who are as anxious to find us as we are to find them. Read Mark 6:7 and answer below.

How did he send His disciples out?

How did He equip them for the mission?

God recognizes the strength that comes from partnership. He will never abandon us nor leave our needs unmet. If you're alone in your organization and feel like the "lone ranger," pray fervently . . . ask

God to lead you to His other faithful followers nearby. Keep on asking, and be alert for His answer. He or she may not be who you expect!

Another huge reason to have partners is for prayer. When you are going to lunch with someone and you're planning to challenge them toward a "next step" in their faith, how awesome it is to be able to quickly ask for and get focused prayer from someone who wants your colleague to take that "next step" as much as you do! We're encouraged to "team up" in praying and we're reminded of God's promises in Matthew 18:19-20.

Will your prayers be answered by the Father when "two or three" ask?

Will Jesus be there with you when "come together in His name"?

Be Careful . . .

There seems to be evidence that a great movement of God is underway in the workplace. Church and ministry leaders like Billy Graham, Henry Blackaby, and a host of others are sensing that something special is happening in the hearts of lay people as they begin to "take their faith to work." Even the secular media has picked up on it, with increased attention to Christian beliefs and practices in the marketplace.

We can rest assured that Satan, the enemy of God, is working overtime to turn this trend around. Let's look at some of the things we'll likely see him do.

1. He will do all he can to embarrass and diminish the impact of successful business people who have been giving God the glory for their success.

2. He will infect the hearts of people in your workplace with skepticism, judgment, jealousy and mistrust of Christians like you . . . people who are "about our Father's business." Your words and actions will be examined as "under a microscope." We must be careful with what we say and do at work so that we always conform to the law and to the policies of our organizations.

3. He will affect circumstances so that stress levels are increased. We all function more poorly when we allow stress to get to us, and that can lead us to say and do things that can get us into trouble.

What are some other evidences that the enemy is active in your workplace?

The Greatest Job Ever!

In survey after survey, employees tell us they care about three things.

1. They want to do work that matters . . . work that has purpose and meaning.

2. They want to belong . . . to feel that they are a part of something special and that someone cares about them.

3. They want to make a contribution . . . to make a difference and not just be "a part of the machinery."

In these weeks, we have reviewed a process that can give every one who works these three things . . . and a lot more! What we do matters for all of eternity—for us and for the people in our sphere of influence. We belong to a great Kingdom that is invisible today but someday, will be visible and tangible. We're valuable members of God's "team" of disciples . . . we're His special agents to our work nation. He cares about us so much that He goes with us every day, in everything we do. And we have the opportunity to make a huge contribution . . . one that we have been uniquely selected for and positioned to make. We have the opportunity to live a great adventure in God-led relationships, and make a difference for Him with people who may never be touched by a church or a vocational minister.

What is our "coefficient of regret" . . . i.e. the likelihood that we will end up with regrets if we choose NOT to try?

Pretty high.

And what is our "probability of success" if we "sign on" to be about our Father's business?

One hundred percent.

We can only fail if we don't try.

God will use whatever you give Him. Give Him a lot . . . no, give Him everything!

Questions for Discussion

1. How did you first identify other "excelling Christians" in your workplace?

2. What are the most significant impediments your organization places between you and your doing the kinds of things you would like to do for His Kingdom in your workplace?

3. How can you "team up" with other excelling Christians without forming a "holy huddle?"

4. Now that you've read *About My Father's Business* and completed this study, what holds you back from being "full on" for Him with the people you work with?

A	B	C	D	E
Apathetic	Beginning (to Search)	Confessing	Developing	Excelling
Doesn't know and doesn't care about spiritual things.	Doesn't know the answers, but is beginning to think there's something there.	Believes that Jesus Christ was God, but you would never know it. Passive!	Seriously committed to Christianity, growing, not ashamed of their faith. Active!	Living out the Christian life and is helping others get there.

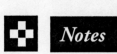

Notes

ABOUT MY

FATHER'S

BUSINESS

TAKING YOUR FAITH TO WORK

LEADER'S GUIDE

About My Father's Business was written by a business person . . . a practitioner who has been blessed with success in the marketplace while actively attempting to influence people for Christ at the same time. The purpose of this study is to inspire and instruct Christians in the workplace to participate in the work of a disciple… a learner and follower of Jesus Christ.

The vision is that a group of individuals . . . probably no more than twelve people, would read the book in weekly "chunks," do the homework assignment, and come to a weekly session to discuss the material. It is anticipated that these participants are believers, but with various levels of spiritual maturity. This is not a study to be taught, but one to be facilitated. People have been "preached at" to share their faith for decades, but what is called for here is a leader who will simply DO what's described in the material and be willing to lead a discussion about it.

The currency of a small group of working people is conversation. The more each person invests, participates, and shares, the more they will be inspired to become active for Christ at work. So, first and foremost, we want to encourage dialogue and participation from everyone.

The study is designed to take seven weeks. Each session can be done in about 1 hour and 15 minutes. Obviously, the sessions can be longer if more time is devoted to review of the material or more in-depth discussion. The homework should take no more than one hour each week, including preparing answers to the discussion questions.

This guide is intended to help you shape the discussion . . . to know some of the answers to the questions that the author had in mind, and to give you a "track to run on" in facilitating the seven sessions

The desired outcome of this study is that everyone who

participates will move from a more passive, "me centered" Christianity, to an active, "others centered" faith. If every participant emerges with a list of people that they are praying for and investing in, for the purpose of helping each to move one step closer to Christ, then your group will have been a smashing success!

Week One — Work, Calling and the Next Step in the "Purpose Driven Life"

Important: distribute the first week's reading material and homework assignment before the first session. This will allow you to immediately jump into the subject. Working people do not want to "waste" a session to pick up their books and have an overview of the study.

Read Pages 13-29 in *About My Father's Business*

Session Outline

1. Begin by having each person introduce themselves, their organization, and their "title." There'll be a few snickers, but it's a sneaky way of having them disclose a little more about what they do.

2. Share the purpose of the group from the introductory material above.

3. Begin the session (and each session) with something like this... "As you did the homework this week, what jumped out at you? Was there any particular concept from the book or homework or any specific Scripture that 'popped onto your radar screen?'"

Then lead the discussion, keeping it on track to the central theme, which is being active for Christ in your work place.

4. Move the discussion toward the Scriptures that instruct us to be disciples . . . missionaries to the "work nation." Here are the Scriptures.

    Matthew 28:19— *Therefore go and make disciples of all nations, baptizing them in the name of the Father and of the Son and of the Holy Spirit.*

    Mark 16:15—*Go into all the world and preach the good news to all creation.*

    Luke 24:47—*and repentance and forgiveness of sins will be preached in his name to all nations, beginning at Jerusalem.*

    John 20:21—*Again Jesus said, "Peace be with you! As the Father has sent me, I am sending you.*

    Acts 1:8—*But you will receive power when the Holy Spirit comes on you; and you will be my witnesses in Jerusalem, and in all Judea and Samaria, and to the ends of the earth.*

5. Reinforce the assignment to write down the four parts of your "story." We'll come back to this in week 4, but it's critical that a Christian be able to tell his own story in an honest, but compelling way.

6. Most people haven't seen the connection between the quality of their secular work and their influence for Christ. Here are the Scriptures and qualities of a good worker from the homework.

a. Proverbs 22:29 — *Be good at your work; develop your skills*

b. Phil. 2:14 — *Have a good attitude at work*

c. Col. 4:1 — *Treat people fairly; do what's right*

d. Col. 4:5-6 — *Be nice to people*

e. I Thess. 4:12 — *Be trustworthy*

f. Col. 3:22-25 — *Accept and respect authority*

g. Eccl. 9:10 — *Work hard when you work*

h. Matt. 5:37 — *Be clear and specific in your communications*

i. Phil. 2:3-4 — *Be humble*

7. Have participants turn to Matthew 16:24. Have someone read the verse and then discuss the "fill in the blanks."

   a. Jesus is in heaven today. If anyone wants to follow Him, in this life and into the next, He'll be called on to deny himself, take up his cross, and follow Jesus.

   b. "Denying yourself" says "I am going to move beyond the "I" focus, (all the things I get from being a Christian) to the "others focus" that Jesus modeled.

   c. The Cross is a symbol of suffering. Jesus suffered on the Cross for others, not for Himself. So "take up your cross" may mean to "suffer personally" for the benefit of others. Investing in relationships that aren't comfortable, but doing so to have influence for Christ, may be a part of "taking up your cross."

d. Follow me into the work "nation" says "I'm going to be on a daily 'mission from God.' I'm going to ask for my daily 'orders' and follow them. I'm going to love, serve, accept and pray for people in my sphere of influence, with the hope that they'll move one step closer to Christ.

8. Review the idea that intentionality correlates with motive, and that God is all about motive. He is more about why we do things than about what we do. Knowing that He is responsible for outcomes narrows our focus . . .we are simply to be on His agenda, focused on relationships for His purposes in order to be about His business fulltime.

9. Go over the discussion questions.

10. Review the first memory verse.

"In the same way, let your light shine before men, that they may see your good deeds and praise your Father in heaven."
MATTHEW 5:16

11. Close in prayer.

Week Two – Intentionality

Read pages 30-55 in *About My Father's Business*

Session Outline

1. Review the key points from week one.

2. Ask the group . . . "As you did the homework this week, what jumped out at you? Was there any particular concept from the book or homework or any specific Scripture that 'popped onto your radar screen?'"

3. Begin by discussing the idea of having two jobs at the same time, using Matthew 6:33 as the roadmap.

   a. *"But seek first his kingdom and his righteousness, and all these things will be given to you as well."*

   b. What does He want us to "seek" first? His kingdom

   c. What does "and His righteousness" mean? He wants us to be righteous ourselves, like Jesus was.

   d. Where does His "kingdom" exist? In the hearts of men.

   e. What does "all these things will be given to you as well" refer to? He's referring to the necessities of life . . . food, clothing and shelter.

   f. Review the paraphrase of Matthew 6:33 which is "Make it your first job (seek first) to be about seeking the hearts of men and women for me, don't forget to seek My righteousness yourself, and I will meet the physical needs of life for you."

4. Reinforce these two key points . . .

   a. Life is defined by relationships; they are the essence of life and aren't optional. What's optional is who we enter into relationships with and for what purpose.

   b. Everyone will spend eternity somewhere. This stuff is important! The eternal destination of our colleagues (and their families) is at stake!

5. Review Colossians 1:10.

   a. God wants us to live a life worthy of the Lord, pleasing Him in every way: bearing fruit in every good work, growing in the knowledge of God.

   b. Reinforce the fact that living our lives in a Christ-like fashion is the necessary "first step" in bearing fruit.

6. Romans 7:15 reminds us of the struggle we have in consistently being about our Father's business. It states . . . *"I do not understand what I do. For what I want to do, I do not do, but what I hate, I do."*

7. Share a little from your own "thank you letter" to God as an example for the group, if you feel led to do so. Be careful of the time, since this part of the discussion can be very hard to manage . . . i.e. it's hard to cut off the sharing here, once it starts.

8. An example of a "blessing" and a "what if" might be . . .

Blessings	What If
Great marriage	*Husband or wife abandoned me*
Nice home	*Home destroyed by fire*
College Education	*Failure to get an education could have left you underemployed and poor.*

Be careful, because some people's blessings may not have come to everyone in the group. But helping people to see God's blessings and protection in their lives can lead them to the humble heart that God can use.

9. James 1:17—*"Every good and perfect gift is from above, coming down from the Father of the heavenly lights, who does not change like shifting shadows."*

10. Matthew 7:11—*"If you, then, though you are evil, know how to give good gifts to your children, how much more will your Father in heaven give good gifts to those who ask him!"*

11. Talk about our new blessings.

   a. John 14:27—*"Peace I leave with you; my peace I give you. I do not give to you as the world gives. Do not let your hearts be troubled and do not be afraid."*

b. Galatians 5:1—*"It is for freedom that Christ has set us free. Stand firm, then, and do not let yourselves be burdened again by a yoke of slavery."*

c. Proverbs 3:3-4—*"Let love and faithfulness never leave you; bind them around your neck, write them on the tablet of your heart. Then you will win favor and a good name in the sight of God and man.*

d. Revelation 4:10-11—*"The twenty-four elders fall down before him who sits on the throne, and worship him who lives for ever and ever. They lay their crowns before the throne and say: 'You are worthy, our Lord and God, to receive glory and honor and power, for you created all things, and by your will they were created and have their being.'"*

12. Go over the discussion questions.

13. Review the memory verse:

"But seek first his kingdom and his righteousness, and all these things will be given to you as well."
   MATTHEW 6:33

14. Close in prayer.

Week Three – Relationships are the Thing!

Read pages 44-59 in *About My Father's Business*

Session Outline

1. Review the key points from week two.

2. Ask the group . . . "As you did the homework this week, what jumped out at you? Was there any particular concept from the book or homework or any specific Scripture that 'popped onto your radar screen?'"

3. John 13:34-35

   a. The command from our "Boss" is to love one another . . . as He has loved us.

   b. He loves us unconditionally . . . we don't have to change to be loved!

4. Discuss the story of Zacchaeus

   a. Jesus communicated acceptance before love (vs. 5)

   b. Jesus required NO CHANGE in behavior from Zacchaeus before He communicated His acceptance.

   c. Zacchaeus made radical changes in His behavior after Jesus accepted him, and after Zacchaeus accepted Jesus. He gave up his dishonest practices and repaid what he had stolen in multiples.

5. The exercise on page 46 is to help us identify our judgmental "hang-ups" and biases. An example might be . . .

Issue Person	*The Issue*	*Your new "acceptance" response*
Bill	*piercings, nose ring*	*eye contact, smile*
Sue	*left her husband*	*ask to lunch*
Bob	*angry at everyone*	*express interest in family*

6. Discuss the intentionality maps.

7. Go over the discussion questions

8. Review the memory verse:

> *"A new command I give you: Love one another. As I have loved you, so you must love one another. By this all men will know that you are my disciples, if you love one another."*
> *JOHN 13:34-35*

9. Close in prayer.

Week Four – Going on the Journey with Them!

Read pages 60-90 in *About My Father's Business*

Session Outline

1. Review the key points from week three.

2. Ask the group . . . "As you did the homework this week, what jumped out at you? Was there any particular concept from the book or homework or any specific Scripture that 'popped onto your radar screen?'"

3. Read Titus 2:10 "*. . . and not to steal from them, but to show that they can be fully trusted, so that in every way they will make the teaching about God our Savior attractive.*"

   a. Believers must be honest in all their dealings, even in the smallest things!

   b. He wants us to show that we can be fully trusted.

   c. If the messenger is trustworthy, then the message has more credibility.

4. Discuss James 1:19-20

   a. We're to be quick to listen.

   b. We're to be slow to speak.

   c. We're to be slow to become angry.

5. 1 Cor. 8:1 says, *"Knowledge puffs up, but love builds up."*

    a. Verse 2 says *"The man who thinks he knows something does not yet know as he ought to know"* . . . ie. he has not yet learned to be humble.

    b. We should have no pressure to "know it all." He's responsible for outcomes. We just need to learn all we can as we go, and trust Him to fill in our gaps.

6. Col. 4:5-6 *"Be wise in the way you act toward outsiders; make the most of every opportunity. Let your conversation be always full of grace, seasoned with salt, so that you may know how to answer everyone."*

    a. We're to be wise.

    b. Our conversations are to be full of grace.

    c. We'll be able to answer everyone.

7. Jesus is the way, the truth and the life. He is the only way to the Father. (John 14:6)

    a. Salvation is found in no one other than Jesus Christ. (Acts 4:12)

8. Go over the discussion questions.

9. Review the memory verse.

    "Then you will know the truth, and the truth will set you free."   JOHN 8:32

10. Close in prayer.

Week Five – Taking THEM on a Journey with YOU!

Read pages 112-143 in *About My Father's Business*

Session Outline

1. Review the key points from week four.

2. Ask the group . . . "*The seed that fell among thorns stands for those who hear, but as they go on their way they are choked by life's worries, riches and pleasures, and they do not mature.*"

3. Discuss Luke 8:14. "*And that which fell among thorns are they, which, when they have heard, go forth, and are choked with cares and riches and pleasures of this life, and bring no fruit to perfection.*"

   a. Cares (which often come from "stuff"), riches, pleasures, ambition, ego, fear . . . all these "choke" faith.

   b. When and where does it happen? Along the way . . . just doing life.

   c. An immature plant struggles to survive in hard times . . . and it almost never bears any fruit.

4. Discuss Matthew 5:13. "*You are the salt of the earth. But if the salt loses its saltiness, how can it be made salty again? It is no longer good for anything, except to be thrown out and trampled by men.*"

a. Jesus called his followers, the disciples the "salt of the earth."

b. Salt that has lost its saltiness is still salt.

c. Salt that's lost its saltiness is useless and gets thrown out . . . back to the "path" where its trampled under foot.

5. Discuss Rev. 3:15-16. *"I know your deeds, that you are neither cold nor hot. I wish you were either one or the other! So, because you are lukewarm--neither hot nor cold--I am about to spit you out of my mouth."*

a. God knows our mediocrity because he knows our deeds.

b. Mediocrity makes God sick . . . literally "to vomit."

c. His reaction is so strong because He loves us so much. Love Him or hate Him, but at least care!

6. Discuss Romans 14:3. *"The man who eats everything must not look down on him who does not, and the man who does not eat everything must not condemn the man who does, for God has accepted him."*

a. We're told not to look down on those who don't subscribe to the same religious practices as we do. This also says to not look down on those who aren't as spiritually mature as us.

b. God has accepted both.

7. Our three assignments from Hebrews 10:23-25. *"Let us hold unswervingly to the hope we profess, for he who promised is faithful. And let us consider how we may spur one another on toward love and good deeds. Let us not give up meeting together, as some are in the habit of doing, but let us encourage one another—and all the more as you see the Day approaching."*

   a. " . . . .hold unswervingly to the hope we profess.

   b. "consider how we may spur one another on toward love and good deeds."

   c. "not give up meeting together."

8. Go over discussion questions

9. Review memory verse.

   "And let us consider how we may spur one another on toward love and good deeds." HEBREWS 10:24

10. Close in prayer.

Week Six – From "It" to "Him"

Read pages 144-154 in *About My Father's Business*

Session Outline

1. Review the key points from week five.

2. Ask the group . . . "As you did the homework this week, what jumped out at you? Was there any particular concept from the book or homework or any specific Scripture that 'popped onto your radar screen?'"

3. Look at Romans 10:9. *"That if you confess with your mouth, 'Jesus is Lord,' and believe in your heart that God raised him from the dead, you will be saved."*

   a. Our first instruction is to confess with our mouth that Jesus is Lord.

   b. We're also reminded that we must believe in our heart that God raised him from the dead to be saved.

4. Discuss Matthew 10:32-33. *"Whoever acknowledges me before men, I will also acknowledge him before my Father in heaven. But whoever disowns me before men, I will disown him before my Father in heaven."*

   a. Jesus promises to acknowledge him before the Father in heaven.

   b. The consequences of disowning Him before men is that He will disown him before the Father in heaven.

5. *Discuss Colossians 2:6-7. "So then, just as you received Christ Jesus as Lord, continue to live in him, rooted and built up in him, strengthened in the faith as you were taught, and overflowing with thankfulness."*

"received Jesus Christ"—means "confessed with our lips and believed in our hearts that Jesus is Lord."

"continue to live in Him"—means you've stuck with it . . . that you have continued in your relationship since you first met Him.

"rooted and built up in Him"—means that you've matured in your faith and in your relationship with Him. You read God's Word, you pray, you're grounded in what you believe and how you live.

"strengthened in your faith as you were taught"—Strength is built through exercise, nourishment, and experience.

"overflowing with thankfulness"—as we mature, we realize in a greater and deeper way, what Christ did for us, what He means to us and how great a sacrifice He made for us. As our gratitude overflows, we want to please Him even more.

6. Discuss John 5:39-40. *"You diligently study the Scriptures because you think that by them you possess eternal life. These are the Scriptures that testify about me, yet you refuse to come to me to have life."*

   a. We can "study the scriptures" but never really experience God. We must come to Him to have life.

7. Eph. 6:18. *"And pray in the Spirit on all occasions with all kinds of prayers and requests. With this in mind, be alert and always keep on praying for all the saints."*

   a. Yes, he means to pray on all occasions.

   b. We can pray prayers of praise, of thanksgiving, request wisdom, request guidance, request intervention, request understanding, confession, requesting mercy….there is an unlimited number of prayers we can offer up to Him.

   c. "Always keep on praying" communicates God's affinity for persistence. He appreciates it in us, because He has to be so persistent (and patient) with us. Is it reasonable? Yes, because God instructs us to "pray without ceasing" in His Word.

   d. God often answers our prayers and we don't even notice. He wants us to look for His hand everywhere, and to be on the alert to other needs where we may be the vehicle He uses to answer someone else's prayer.

8. Discuss John 14:26. *"But the Counselor, the Holy Spirit, whom the Father will send in my name, will teach you all things and will remind you of everything I have said to you."*

   a. The Counselor will be sent in Jesus' name.

   b. The Counselor will teach us all things.

   c. The Counselor will remind us of the words of Jesus.

up. But pity the man who falls and has no one to help him up! Also, if two lie down together, they will keep warm. But how can one keep warm alone? Though one may be overpowered, two can defend themselves. A cord of three strands is not quickly broken.”

a. We will have a good return.

b. We can help each other when we fall down.

c. We can keep each other warm (spiritually).

d. We can join together to defend ourselves.

6. Discuss Mark 6:7. *“Calling the Twelve to him, he sent them out two by two and gave them authority over evil spirits.”*

a. He sent them out two by two.

b. He gave them authority over evil spirits.

c. Their mission seems to have been to cast out evil spirits. Jesus gave them exactly what they needed to accomplish their mission . . . no more and no less. That’s what He will do for us.

11. Discuss Matthew 18:19-20. *“Again, I tell you that if two of you on earth agree about anything you ask for, it will be done for you by my Father in heaven. For where two or three come together in my name, there am I with them.”*

a. Our prayers will be answered when “two or three” ask.

b. Jesus will be there when we come together in His name.

12. Talk about some common evidences of Satan in the workplace.

   —A culture of deceit and a lack of truthfulness.

   —Rampant sensuality and use of pornography.

   —Angry coworkers who hate their bosses and their jobs.

   —Low trust environments where it's "everyone for himself."

13. Go over the discussion questions

14. Review the memory verse.

   "Have I not commanded you? Be strong and courageous. Do not be terrified; do not be discouraged, for the Lord your God will be with you wherever you go."
   JOSHUA 1:9

15. Close in prayer.